QUILTED ANIMALS

Continuous Line Patterns

American Quilter's Society
P. O. Box 3290 • Paducah, KY 42002-3290
www.AQSquilt.com

Marta Amundson

Located in Paducah, Kentucky, the American Quilter's Society (AQS) is dedicated to promoting the accomplishments of today's quilters. Through its publications and events, AQS strives to honor today's quiltmakers and their work and to inspire future creativity and innovation in quiltmaking.

EDITOR: BARBARA SMITH
GRAPHIC DESIGN: ELAINE WILSON
COVER DESIGN: MICHAEL BUCKINGHAM
PHOTOGRAPHY: CHARLES R. LYNCH, UNLESS INDICATED OTHERWISE

Library of Congress Cataloging-in-Publication Data
Amundson, Marta
     Quilted animals : continuous line patterns / by Marta Amundson.
      p. cm.
      ISBN 1-57432-797-6
      1. Quilting--Patterns.   2. Appliqué--Patterns.   3. Animals in art.
   I. Title.
      TT835 .A4953   2002
      746.46'041--dc21

                        2002004845

Additional copies of this book may be ordered from the American Quilter's Society, PO Box 3290, Paducah, KY 42002-3290, or online at www.AQSquilt.com.

Copyright © 2002, Marta Amundson

ON THE COVER: There's No Place Like Home

DEDICATION

For my husband, Larry, who suffers intermittent domestic mayhem and compromised cuisine without complaint. His support, accepting nature, and unconditional love make it possible for me to be an artist and animal advocate.

MINNESOTA MUTANTS
60" x 53"

ACKNOWLEDGMENT My thanks to Diana and Kevin for their help with my text.

"In the end, we will conserve only what we love, we will love only what we understand, and we will understand only what we are taught."

Conservationist Baba Dioum

CONTENTS

INTRODUCTION

You can't live in a place like Wyoming and ignore the environment. Some people may not care about what happens to a rare species of fish or a little bird…or if wolves are again a part of the Yellowstone ecosystem. However, I really do care.

In addition to my wildlife quilts, I make quilts about women's issues, world politics, my dreams, and the environment. On the back of each quilt, I write a statement on fabric. This gives me the opportunity to share my voice with the public and reinforce that voice with a visual image that they can remember. My goal is not to change anyone's point of view but rather to distinctly express my own.

My inspiration can come from an early morning in the rain forest canopy of Puerto Rico, a camel saddle in Egypt, or looking for Bengal Tigers from the back of an elephant in Nepal. I draw composite animals from my photographs that become appliquéd or quilted silhouettes in my quilts.

This pattern book is about the wildlife I love. Not everyone has the opportunity to go to exotic places or even to a zoo. Not all people who make quilts can draw, but that's okay. I'm sure that with a little imagination and practice you will be able to use a simple roll of freezer paper and my drawings in a creative way all your own. You can use the animals in borders or as appliqué. You can hand quilt them or use your sewing machine. You can enlarge or reduce the designs with a computer scanner or a photocopy machine. You can reverse the images and make them walk in different directions. You can make the images meet nose to nose or tail to tail. You can add other designs like leaves and vines between the animals, or you can fill in the spaces with more than one type of animal.

As a variation, you can arrange the animals in a kaleidoscope pattern to fill plain blocks with what seems like very complex quilting. Actually, it is easy! You can also create amazing appliqué blocks like the ones in the quilt shown on the cover.

Keep in mind that the quilts in this book represent 12 years of my artistic development. You can see a progression from simple quilts like BEAM ME UP, SCOTTY to the more complex ADIOS AMIGOS. Begin quilting where you are, with who you are, and your own growth will be evident in each new quilt you make.

Continuous line quilting is fast and fun. With practice, you will be able to control your stitch length, but don't expect a miracle the first time you lower your feed dogs and give it a go. Take the time to make a quilted book cover or two before you start in on the borders of a quilt. Give yourself time to play and explore. Not everything you make needs to be a masterpiece. With practice you will develop skill and confidence, but in the beginning you need to invest energy in the learning process. Machine quilting is like playing the piano. You start with "Chopsticks" and progress to Chopin.

Your first step starts the journey.

CONTINUOUS LINE QUILTING

Most quilters know that for a quilt to hang true and square on a wall or bed, the amount of quilting should be of about the same density in every area of the quilt. The quilting in the borders should not be an afterthought. With this in mind, I started to experiment with some of my animal templates. Previously, I used an animal as a single element by quilting around each one separately. When I got the idea of placing them nose to tail in a line in the border, it was a eureka moment! You see, I am not fond of knotting and burying the thread ends between the quilt layers, and quilting my animals in a line means I only need to knot my threads at the beginning and ending of each line. With the animals nose to tail, I can sew over all of their backs, then turn and do their feet and bellies.

Quilters love freezer paper. It is commonly used for appliqué patterns and as a stabilizer for machine appliqué. I also use freezer paper as template material for hand and machine quilting. I cut the animal shapes, found in the borders of my work, from freezer paper so they can be easily spaced around the perimeter of my quilt. I iron them down, lower the feed dogs, and use the free-motion foot on my machine to sew around them. Joining the animal templates nose to tail is an option that makes the quilting go faster.

DETERMINING ANIMAL SIZE

First, determine the approximate size of the animal you need by measuring the width of your border. Leave at least a ½" to 1" margin with the animal centered in the middle of the border's width. If the pattern you want to use is too large or small, you can change the size on a photocopy machine or with a scanner and computer.

After determining the width needed for the pattern, you can adjust the length to fit your space by elongating or shortening the animal when you trace it. You can be precise and use math to determine the length of your pattern, or you can "eyeball" it like I do. You may even decide that another animal shape would fit better, so just experiment until you get it the way you want.

MAKING MULTIPLE TEMPLATES

✦ With the right-size copy, trace the animal on a single piece of freezer paper.

✦ Cut seven more pieces of freezer paper about the same size and stack the pieces shiny side down.

✦ With the drawing on top, use a dry, medium-hot iron to fuse the eight layers of paper together only around the perimeter. **Be careful not to touch the iron to the inside of the animal shape.**

✦ Cut out the animal shape through all eight layers (Fig. 1). Then separate the layers to produce eight templates (Fig. 2, page 8).

FIG. 1. Cut all eight layers of freezer paper at once.
PHOTO: MARTA AMUNDSON

FIG. 2. Separate the layers.

FIG. 3. Arrange and iron the templates on your border.

FIG. 4. To start stitching, pull the bobbin thread to the top.

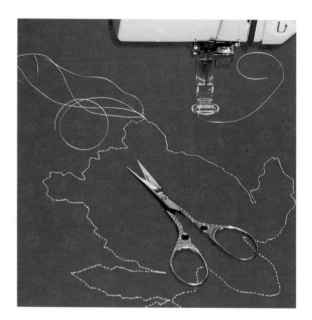

FIG. 5. At the end of the row, pull the bobbin thread to the top, make a knot, then bury the thread ends in the batting. PHOTOS: MARTA AMUNDSON

USING TEMPLATES

✦ Arrange the templates on your quilt border so they touch and iron them in place (Fig. 3). You may need to cut more templates or use the ones you have more than once. Spacing is important, so be sure to take your time.

FREE-MOTION QUILTING

✦ Set your machine for free-motion. In the needle use a thread that contrasts with the quilt top fabric. In the bobbin use a thread that matches the backing fabric.

✦ Sew a little practice square on a small quilt sandwich to check your stitch tension. The stitches should be locking in the middle of the batt, not on the top or bottom layer. If you are using two different thread colors, it is easy to see when this happens. Usually for free-motion quilting you loosen the top tension slightly. Take time to make the stitches balance before you start sewing.

✦ Start by pulling the bobbin thread to the top (Fig. 4). Then put your machine in the needle-down mode, if you have that feature.

✦ Quilt along the animal shape until you come to the place where it touches the next animal. Instead of completing the one you are working on, continue over the top of the next one and the tops of the shapes that follow.

✦ When you reach the end of your templates, quilt back the other way, completing all the animals that you started.

✦ Pull all of your threads to the surface of the quilt top (Fig. 5). Tie the knots and bury them in the layers with your hand sewing needle. I use one of the easy-thread needles with a notch in the top instead of an eye.

✦ Peel off the templates and use them on the next border. Repeat until the borders are complete.

KALEIDOSCOPE PATTERNS

When I made the quilt on the cover, I used the basic method of cutting out the animal shapes from freezer paper and ironing them on fabric, which I later appliquéd. If you want to machine quilt this type of kaleidoscope pattern in a plain block instead of appliquéing it, that is easy to do.

✦ Determine the size of your block and cut out a piece of freezer paper the same size.

✦ Fold the paper in half, then in half again, to make quarter folds.

✦ To make eighths, fold the quarter square into a triangle as shown in Fig. 6.

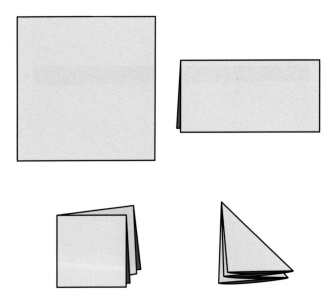

FIG. 6. Fold the square into fourths and then into a triangle.

Fig. 7. (a) dolphin quilting design.

✦ Make an animal template the size needed for the block and fit it on the top one-eighth section. Be sure the animal touches the folded edges in at least one or two places on each side of the triangle (Figs. 7a and 7b). Trace the animal on the triangle section.

✦ Use the tip of your iron to touch the negative spaces around the animal. Be careful not to touch the iron inside the animal shape. **This step will fuse the layers of freezer paper around the perimeter of the animal so that the layers won't shift when you cut.**

✦ Cut the animal out through all the layers, leaving the layers joined where the animal touches the folds.

✦ Mark positioning guidelines on your block by drawing an X in chalk from corner to corner on both diagonals. Open your animal "snowflake" and position the cut-out on the block by aligning the paper folds with the X. Iron the template in place.

✦ Follow the freezer-paper outline as you quilt around the connected animal shapes. Bury your thread tails neatly when you have finished sewing the outline.

An animal's mirror image is formed when two shiny sides of freezer paper are cut face to face. Keep this in mind when you want to make animal opposites in your borders.

Fig. 7. (b) coyote quilting design.

Photos: Marta Amundson

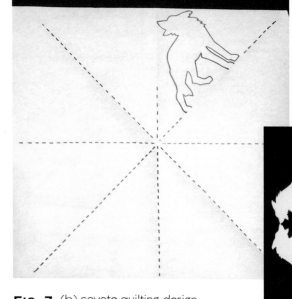

APPLIQUÉ METHODS

There is more than one way to cut up a chicken and more than one way to appliqué one piece of fabric onto another. Before you select a method, you need to ask yourself some questions.

✦ What am I making? Will it be washed often?

✦ How do I want it to feel? If it is a wallhanging, it can be stiff, but if it is a bed or baby quilt, it should have a soft hand when completed.

✦ How do I want it to look? Do I want the hard edge of machine satin stitch or the less defined traditional look of hand appliqué?

✦ How complicated are the shapes that I want to portray?

Here are four appliqué methods and some variations for you to consider:

CLASSIC HAND APPLIQUÉ

This technique maintains the soft hand of the fabric, and it is a great method if you are stranded on an island without your sewing machine, but not so good if the shapes are highly detailed.

✦ Trace your appliqué shape on lightweight card stock, such as an old file folder, to make a template. Cut out the template shape on the traced line.

✦ Place the template face down on the wrong side of the fabric and draw around the template with a pencil. Cut the fabric piece, adding an extra ¼" by eye as you cut for a turn-under allowance.

✦ Spray starch the appliqué piece and put it face down on your ironing board. Center the template, also face down, on top of the appliqué piece.

✦ Using a dry, medium-hot iron, turn and press the allowance over the edge of the template, clipping as required (Fig. 8).

✦ Carefully remove the template and pin the appliqué piece in position on your background fabric.

✦ Appliqué the piece with small, hidden hand stitches, about ¹⁄₁₆" apart.

✦ Leaving a ¼" allowance, cut away the background fabric from underneath the appliqué (Fig. 9, page 12). Press (Fig. 10, page 12).

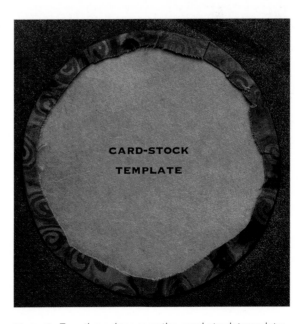

CARD-STOCK TEMPLATE

FIG. 8. Turn the edges over the card-stock template.

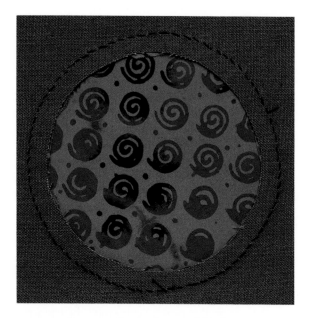

FIG. 9. Cut away the background fabric.

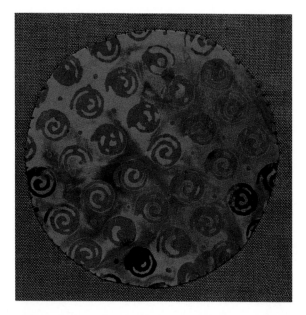

FIG. 10. Press the appliqué from the top.

HAND APPLIQUÉ WITH FREEZER PAPER

Like the previous method, this one also maintains a soft hand. No spray starch or pins are needed, and the steps are about the same as for classic hand appliqué.

✦ Trace your appliqué shape on the dull side of a piece of freezer paper and cut out the shape.

✦ Iron the freezer paper shape on the front of the appliqué fabric. Cut around it, leaving a ¼" seam allowance by eye.

✦ Peel the pattern from the front.

✦ Place the freezer paper pattern, shiny side up, on the wrong side of the appliqué fabric.

✦ Clip the seam allowance as needed as you iron the edges over the paper, where they will stick (Fig. 11).

✦ Iron the freezer-paper template and the appliqué piece onto your background fabric.

FREEZER PAPER

FIG. 11. Turn the fabric edges and iron them onto the freezer paper.

◆ Appliqué the piece to the background with small, hidden stitches about every 1/16".

◆ Leaving a 1/4" seam allowance, cut away the background fabric from underneath the appliqué piece, then pull out the freezer paper. Press.

MACHINE APPLIQUÉ WITH FREEZER PAPER

This method maintains a soft hand, but it is best used with simple shapes.

◆ Cut two same-sized squares (or rectangles) of freezer paper about 1" larger than the shape to be appliquéd.

◆ Cut a square of appliqué fabric the same size as the freezer-paper squares.

◆ On the dull side of one of the freezer-paper pieces, draw your appliqué shape but do not cut it.

◆ Iron the shiny side of the plain freezer paper square on the wrong side of the background fabric

in the area to receive the appliqué.

◆ Place the appliqué fabric square, right side up, on top of the background.

◆ Iron the freezer-paper square with the drawing on top of the appliqué fabric square.

◆ Pin the appliqué in the middle of the background through all the layers. You now have a sandwich with the freezer-paper square on the bottom stuck to the background fabric, and the appliqué fabric square stuck to the freezer paper with the drawing on the top (Fig. 12).

◆ With small free-motion sewing machine stitches, sew along the outline of your drawn shape (Fig. 13).

◆ Tear and peel away the top freezer paper.

◆ With appliqué scissors, cut away the extra appliqué fabric from the outside of the shape as close as you can get to the stitching (Fig. 13).

FREEZER PAPER
FABRIC FOR SHAPE
BACKGROUND FABRIC
FREEZER PAPER

FIG. 12. Appliqué sandwich.

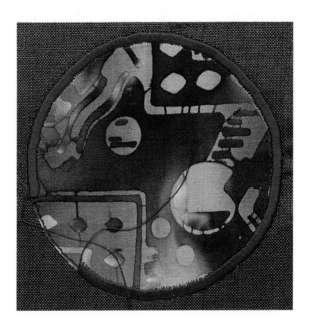

FIG. 13. Satin stitch on foundation.

FIG. 14. Cut away the background fabric.

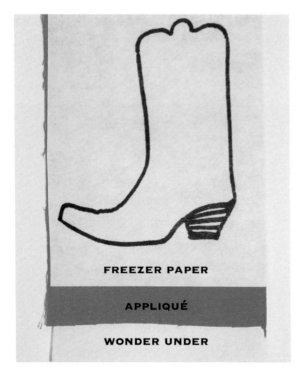

FREEZER PAPER

APPLIQUÉ

WONDER UNDER

FIG. 15. Cut out the shape through all layers.

✦ Satin stitch the outline of the shape, pulling your thread ends to the back and tying them off when you are finished.

✦ Tear and peel away the bottom layer of freezer paper.

✦ With appliqué scissors, cut away the background fabric from underneath the appliqué piece, leaving about ⅛" of fabric beyond the stitching (Fig. 14).

COWGIRL APPLIQUÉ

Use cowgirl appliqué if you are in a hurry and don't mind that the pieces will be a bit stiff. With this easy method, you can make detailed shapes and use many layers of fabric to create definition and dimension. Most of the appliqué on my quilts is made this way. If I have to appliqué over seams in the background, I add a layer of fusible fleece to the sandwich so that the seams will not show through the appliqué.

To protect your ironing board cover from accidents with the fusible material, you can work on a large piece of freezer paper adhered to the cover.

✦ Cut a square (or rectangle) of freezer paper that is about 1" larger than the shape to be appliquéd.

✦ On the dull side of the freezer-paper square, draw your appliqué shape but do not cut it out.

✦ Cut a square of appliqué fabric the same size as the freezer-paper square.

✦ Cut a square of fusible material that is slightly smaller than the appliqué fabric square.

✦ Following the fusible manufacturer's directions, press the fusible to the wrong side of the appliqué fabric square.

✦ Before peeling away the fusible backing, iron the freezer-paper square with your drawing to the front side of the appliqué fabric square.

✦ Following the lines on your drawing, cut out the appliqué shape, through all layers (Fig. 15).

✦ Peel away the freezer paper from the front and the backing paper from the other side of your appliqué piece.

✦ Fuse the appliqué shape in place on the background.

✦ Secure the appliqué with a narrow machine satin stitch (Fig. 16).

✦ Pull the thread ends to the back and tie them together.

✦ Add any thread details, like eyes and ears, with free-motion machine embroidery.

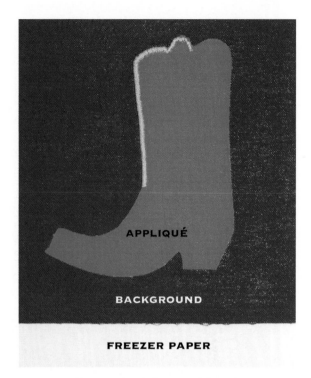

FIG. 16. Use a satin stitch around the edges.

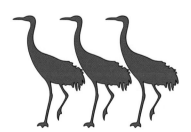

MINSTREL OF THE DEEP

45" x 45"

Humpbacks are 40- to 50-foot-long baleen whales found in all oceans. It is the lone humpback male that sings. At one time, these animals were one of the most abundant large whales worldwide. Humpbacks were hunted extensively through the 1900s, reducing them to alarmingly low numbers. In 1966, they were declared an endangered species and protected. Today, growing numbers of humpback whales are repopulating former ranges, but their continued prosperity depends on human consideration. (*Wild Whales,* 1987)

WHALE

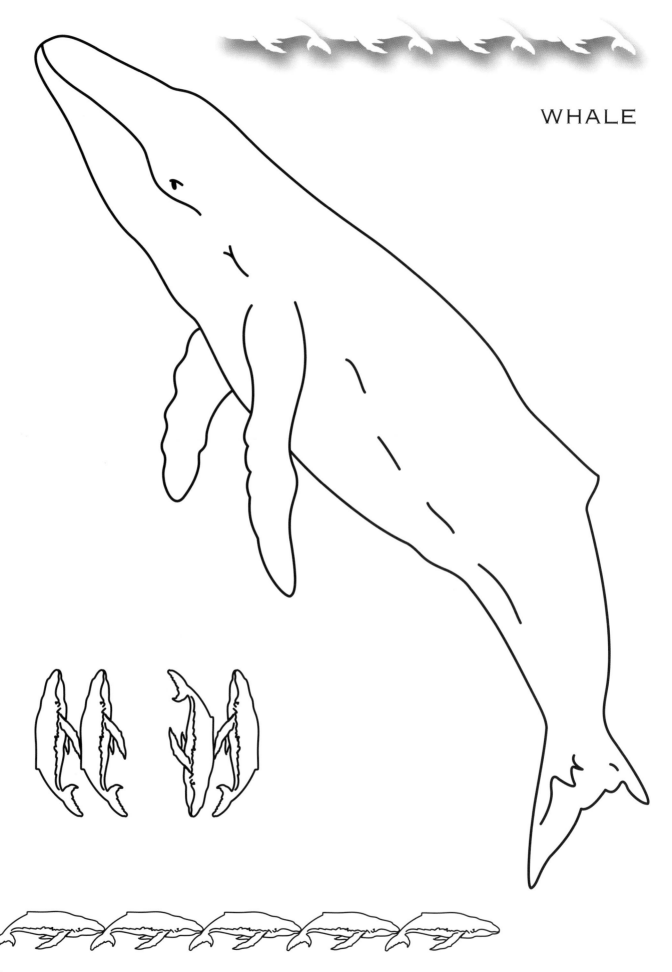

WHALE

BEAM ME UP, SCOTTY

43" x 43"

Dolphins are toothed whales that have a distinct beak and conical teeth. They are found in almost all seas and also in some river systems. Like bats, they possess a special sense called echolocation that helps them navigate and find food at great depths. Although most dolphins are not considered endangered, some dolphin species, such as the Vaquita off Mexico and several of the river dolphins of Asia and South America, are in real danger of extinction. Thousands of dolphins die each year when they become entangled in fishing nets and drown. Industries that dump chemicals and toxins into their environment contribute to habitat destruction. Scientists continue to study dolphins and their habits so that they can better protect them.

TROUT

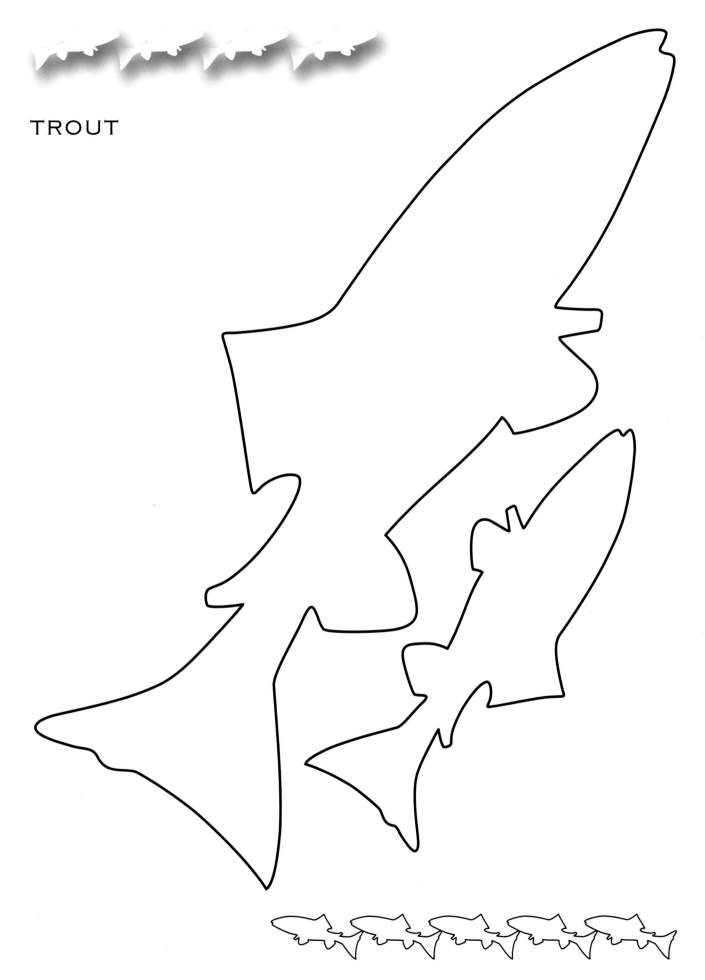

TROUT

TELL ME WHERE THE RHINOS ARE

53" x 67"

Today there are only five species of rhino left, two African and three Asian. All are endangered. Because of the unfounded belief among Asian groups that powdered rhino horn is an aphrodisiac, the market for medicines made from rhino horn encourages poaching. With the modern alternative Viagra, the demand for rhino horn may diminish. In the meantime, trade sanctions on the illegal trade of animals, plants, and associated products are enforced by the U.S. government and the 120 other nations who have an agreement with the Convention on International Trade in Endangered Species. (*Newsweek,* 1993)

RHINO

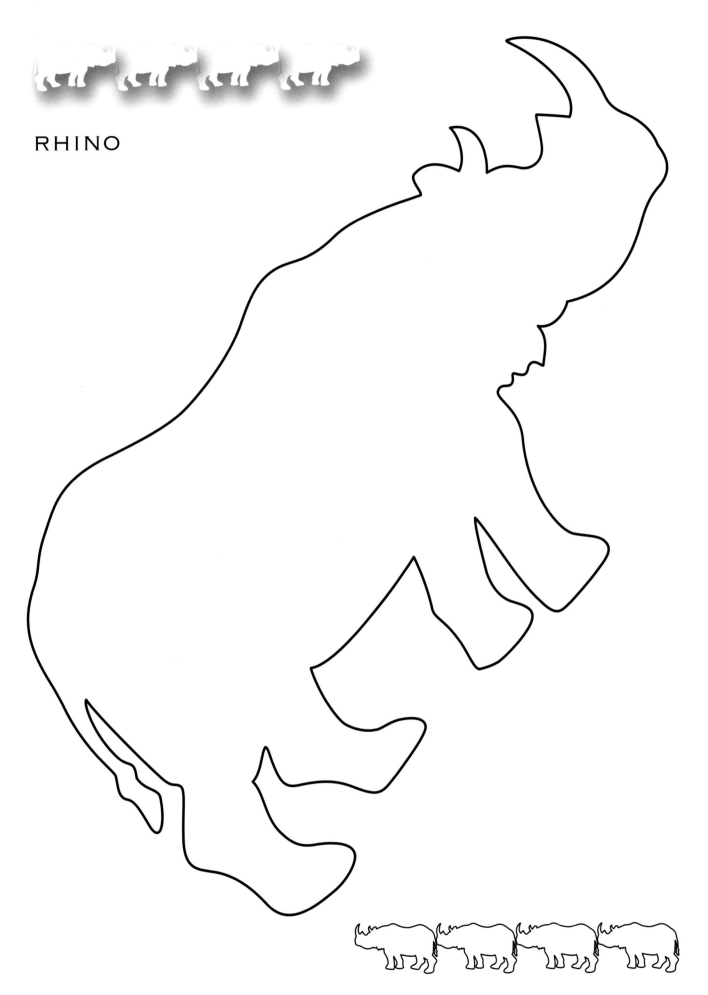

ELEPHANT WALK

55" x 66"

In an effort to make life more normal for their elephants, the keepers at London Zoo take them for long walks around the grounds. When we keep wild animals in captivity, it is important to make their environment a pleasure, not a prison. Too often, captivity damages the mental health of wild animals. Zoo keepers try hard to find creative ways to stimulate animals and help them enjoy life.

CARIBOU

CARIBOU

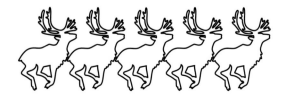

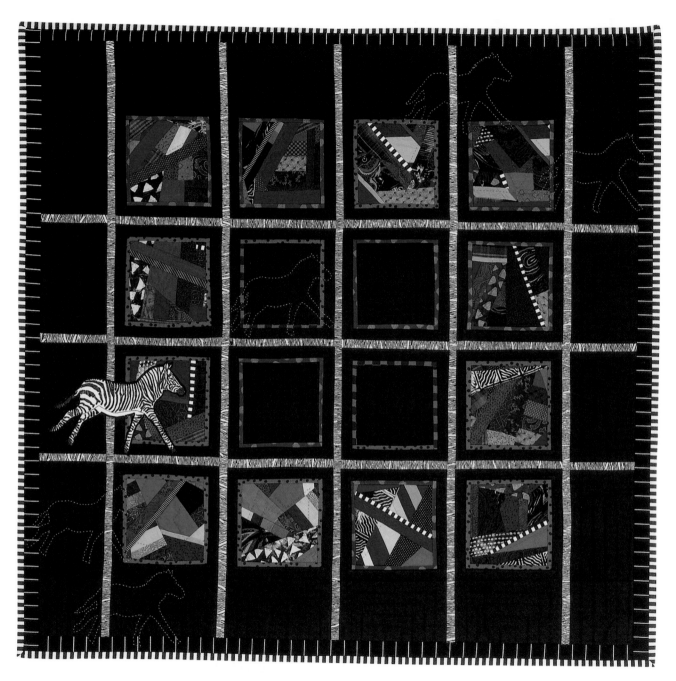

HORSE OF ANOTHER COLOR

45" x 43"

Mountain Zebra National Park was created to stem the loss of grazing land and water holes that have been fenced off by farmers and ranchers in South Africa. Nearly extinct in 1945, Cape mountain zebras now number more than 450. With stripes that resemble human finger prints, each zebra coat design is unique. (*National Geographic,* December 1990)

ZEBRA

ZEBRA

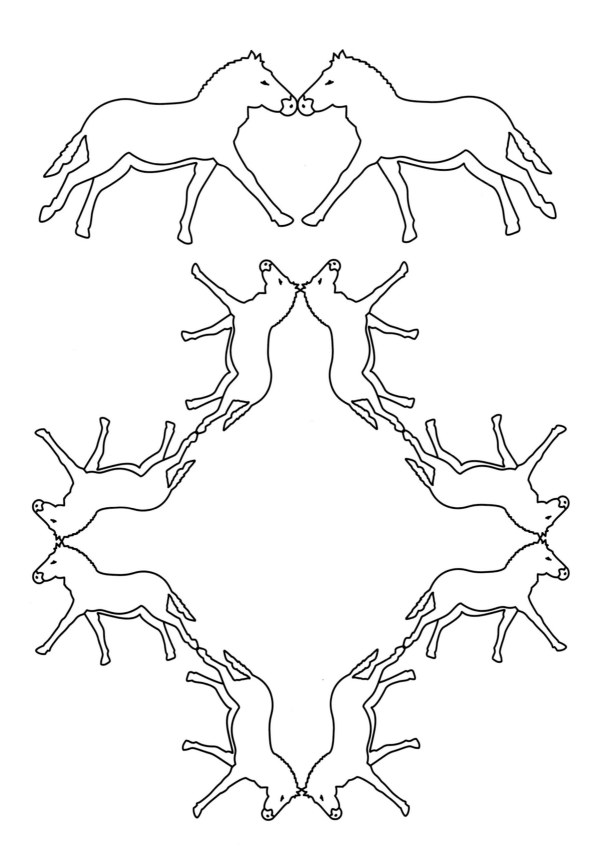

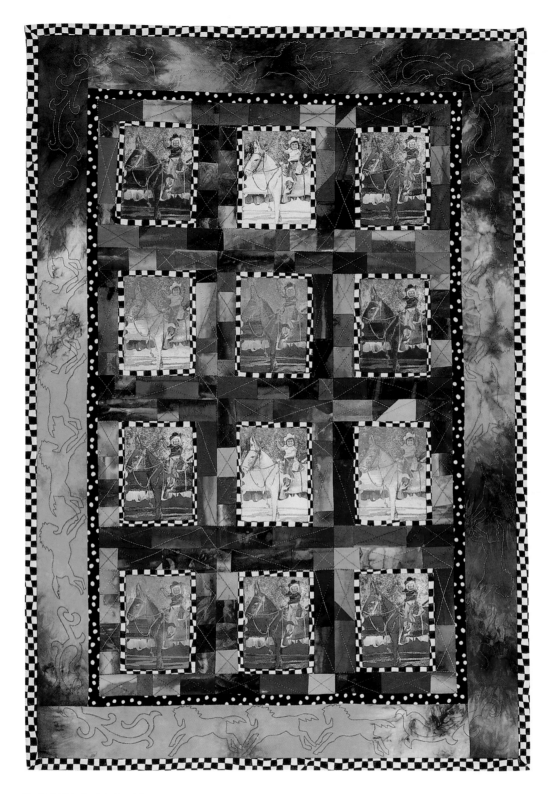

COWGIRL WANNABE

24" x 34"

Even as a very young child, I wanted to be a cowgirl. I aspired to the raw courage, independence, and stubborn daring required to follow my dreams. You don't really need a horse or lariat to be a cowgirl, only a strong will, an obstinate streak, self-reliance, and skill.

HORSE

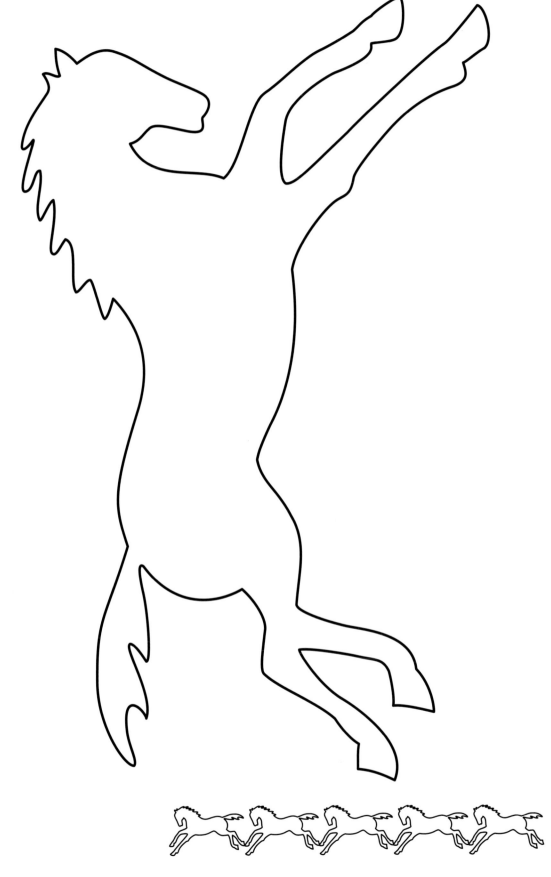

HORSE

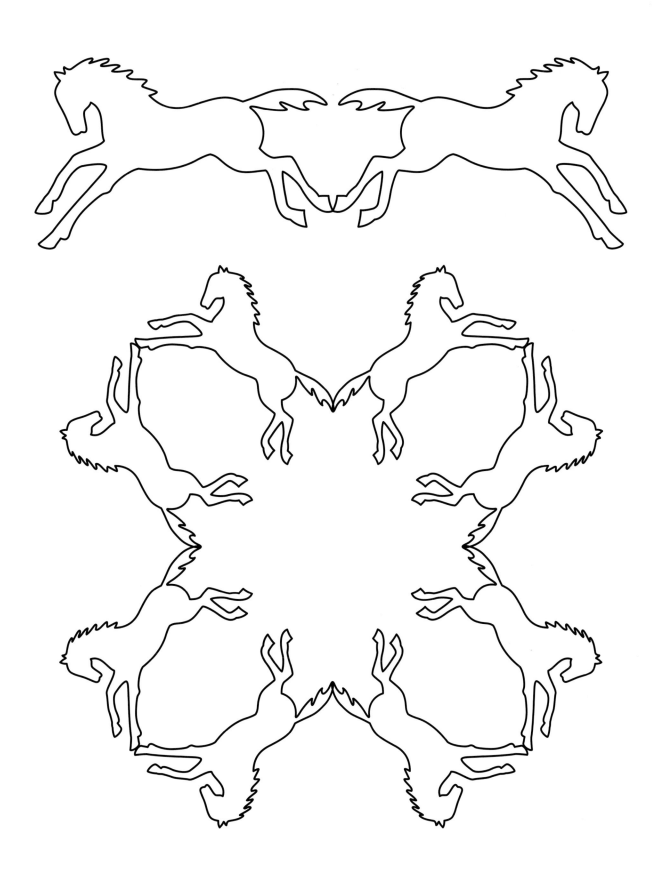

BUFFALOING IN A HOUSE DIVIDED

43" x 64"

Propsed budget refrom shut down the government and cost taxpayers millions in December 1995 and January 1996. Most of what went on in Congress amounted to political posturing for the 1996 fall election. In the words of this cowgirl, they were Buffaloing in a House Divided.

BUFFALO

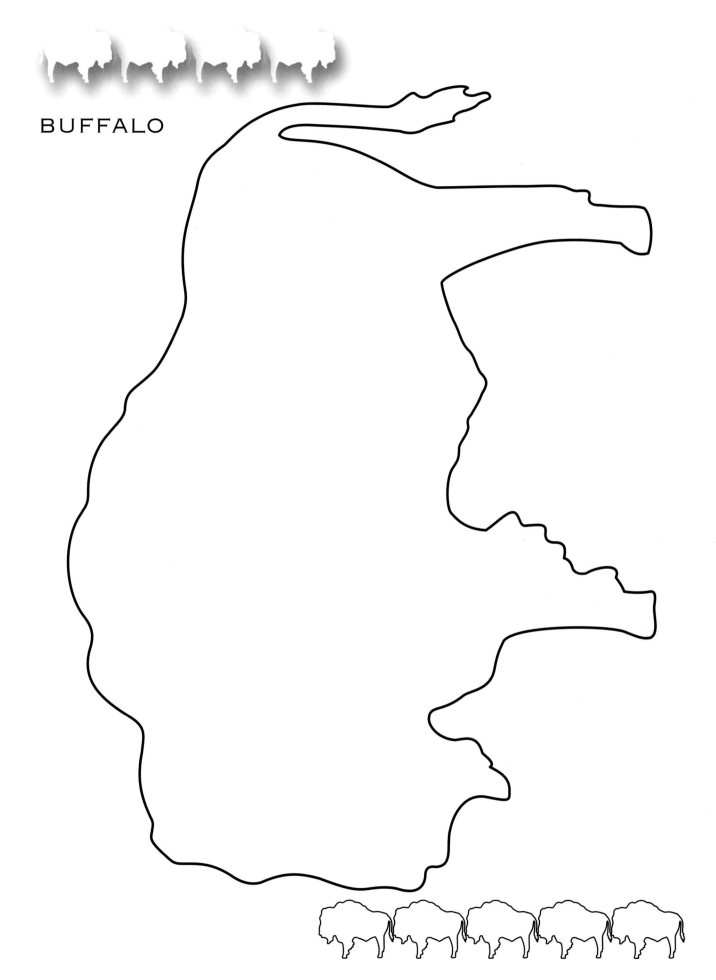

BUFFALO

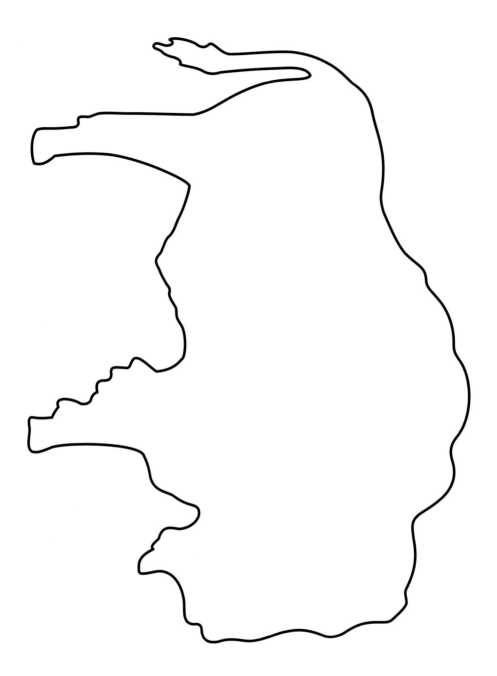

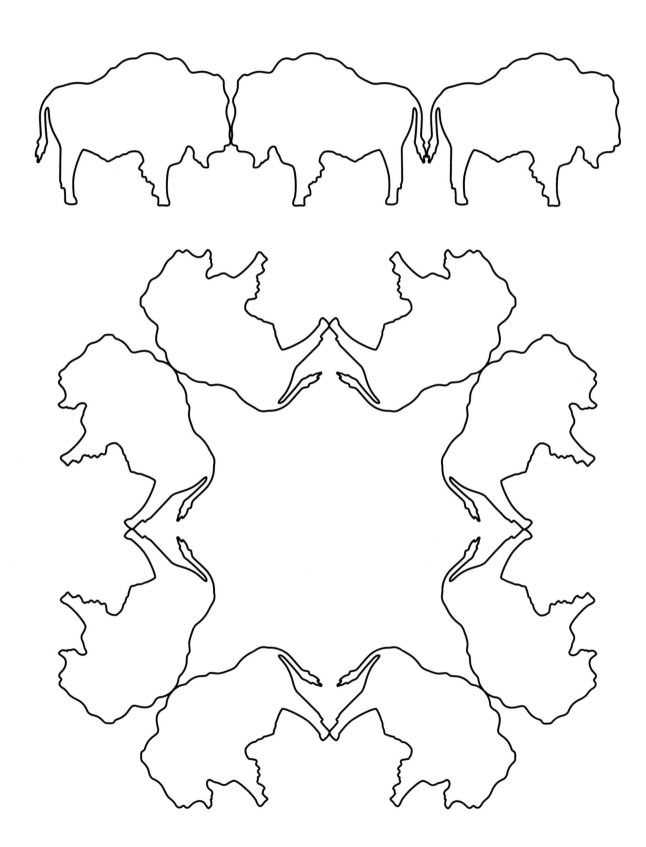

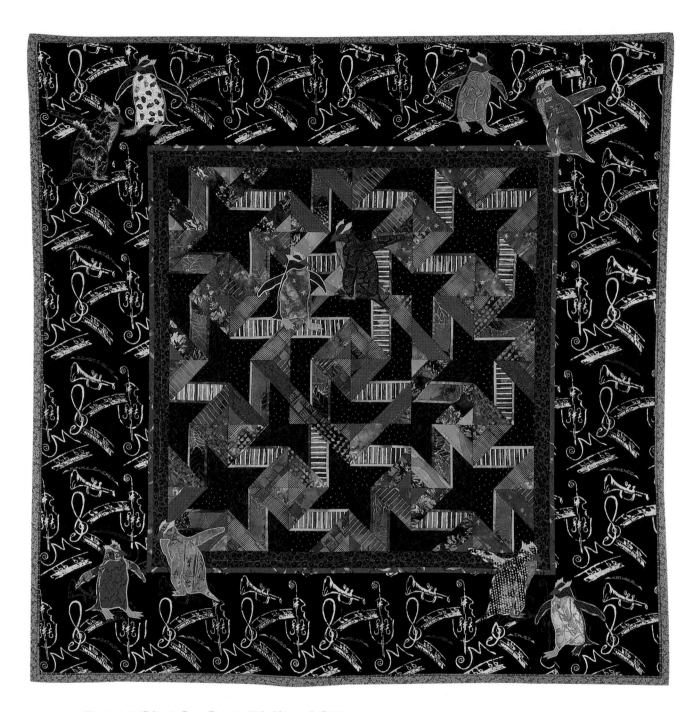

DANCING ON THIN ICE

61" x 61"

Erect-crested penguins live off the coast of New Zealand on the Antipodes and Bounty islands. Scientists believe that their recent low birth rate is due to a depleted food supply, most likely caused by global warming. Other penguin species face threats from oil spills, overfishing, and predation by introduced animals. (Environmental News Bulletin Board, January 1997)

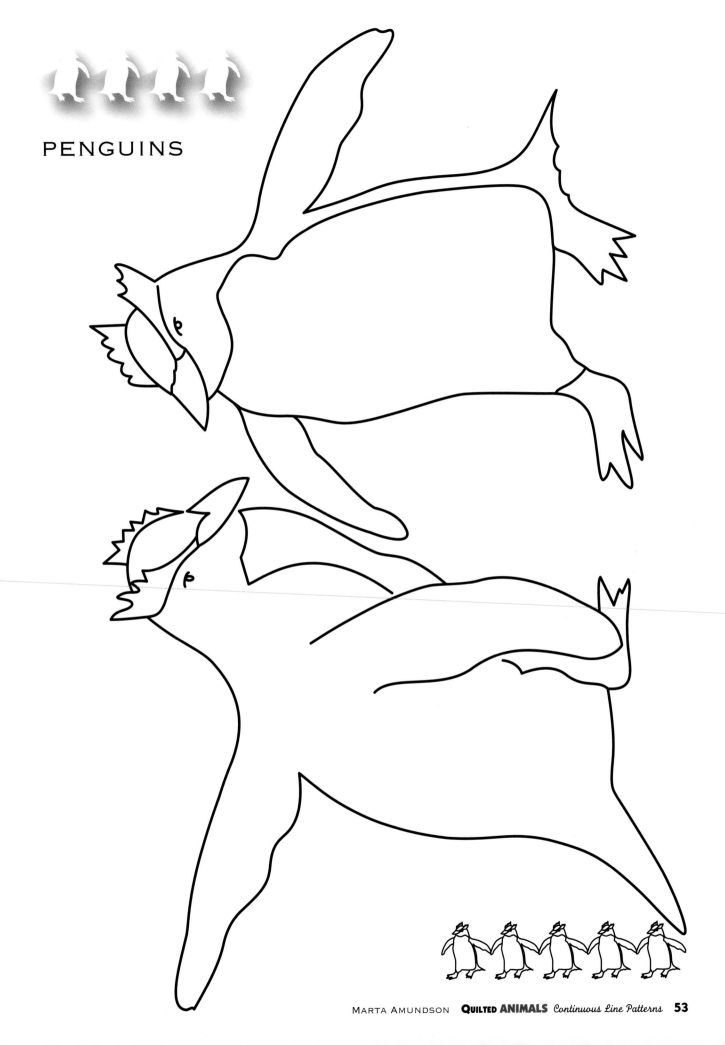

PENGUINS

PENGUINS

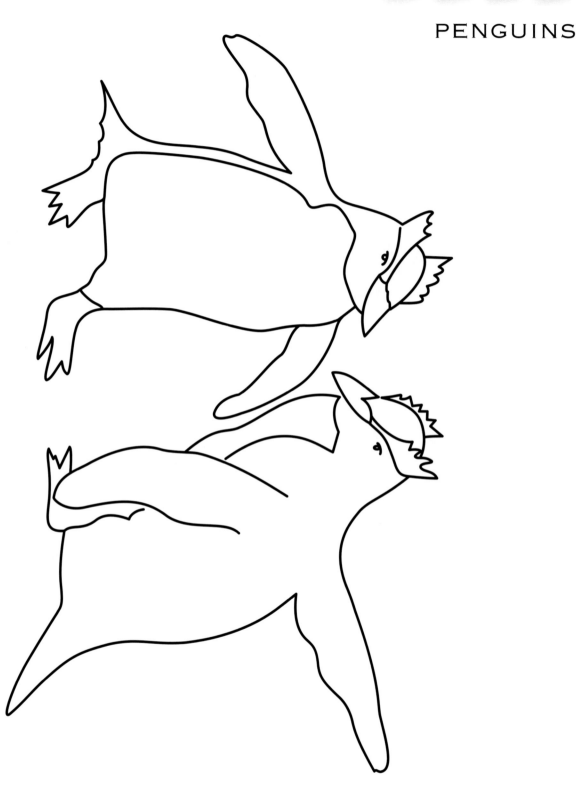

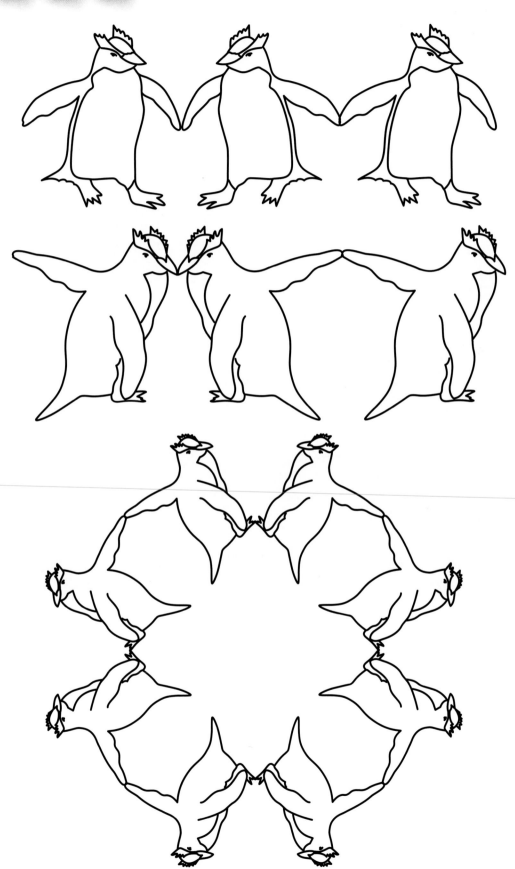

FEATHERED TRIBE FOR A NEW MILLENNIUM

42" x 42"

I'll never forget our excitement when we spotted a whooping crane for the first time. She flew over with a group of sandhill cranes so close that we could almost touch her. She returned the following year and spent the spring and summer with us. Over the last 50 years, a combination of strict legal protection, habitat preservation, and continuous international cooperation between Canada and the United States has allowed the wild population to increase steadily from 15 individuals in 1940–1941 to more than 250 birds. (US Fish and Wildlife website, January 2000)

CRANE

CRANE

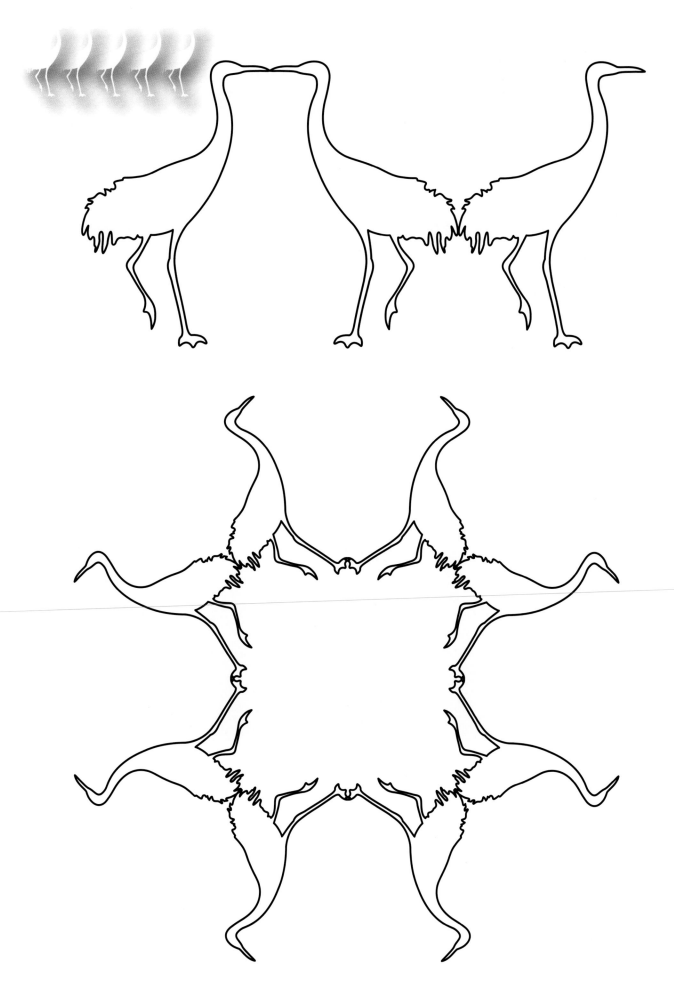

GO TO SLEEP MY LITTLE BAT

62" x 70"

The Ozark big-eared bat was listed as endangered in 1979. With a population of only 1,000, its distribution is limited to a small area in northeast Oklahoma. Echo location allows bats to "see" with their ears. A bat closing in on an insect can emit 200 bursts of sound in a second and analyze the returning signals. Because one bat can eat 500 mosquitoes an hour, in my eyes, they are nature's perfect pesticide.

BAT

BAT

ALMOST PARADISE

63" x 63"

Australia is home to more than one million animal and plant species. About 85% of flowering plants, 84% of mammals, more than 45% of birds and 89% of inshore fish are endemic – that is, they are found only in Australia. Changes in native habitat as a result of human activity have put many of these species at risk. Over the last two hundred years, many have become extinct. For the existing species of plants and animals whose survival is threatened, a range of conservation measures are in place. The Commonwealth of Australia is working in partnership with its states to insure the protection of their remaining native species. (www.ea.gov.au)

ALLIGATOR

KANGAROO

KOALA

KOOKABURRA

PLATYPUS

OUTNUMBERED BY LITTLE FOXES

42" x 48"

Everyone has those little problems that niggle here and there. I find that a trip to the sewing machine or an evening with a needle can help focus my creativity to foil those enigmas that unbalance my life. I try to find time every day for sewing so that I can best maintain my mental health. Take my advice – never be too busy to quilt or you may find yourself outnumbered by little foxes.

FOX

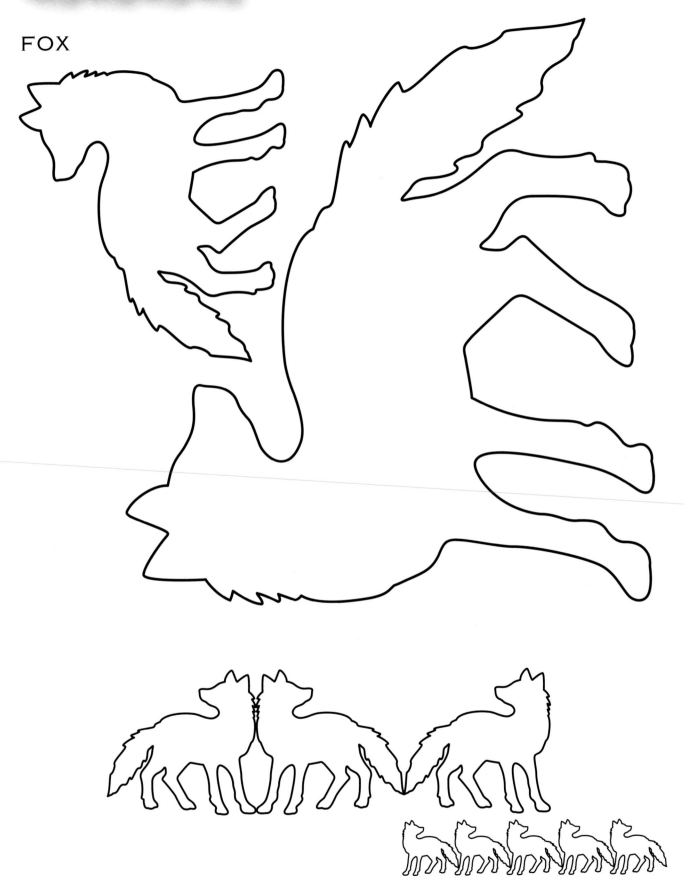

FOX AND RABBIT

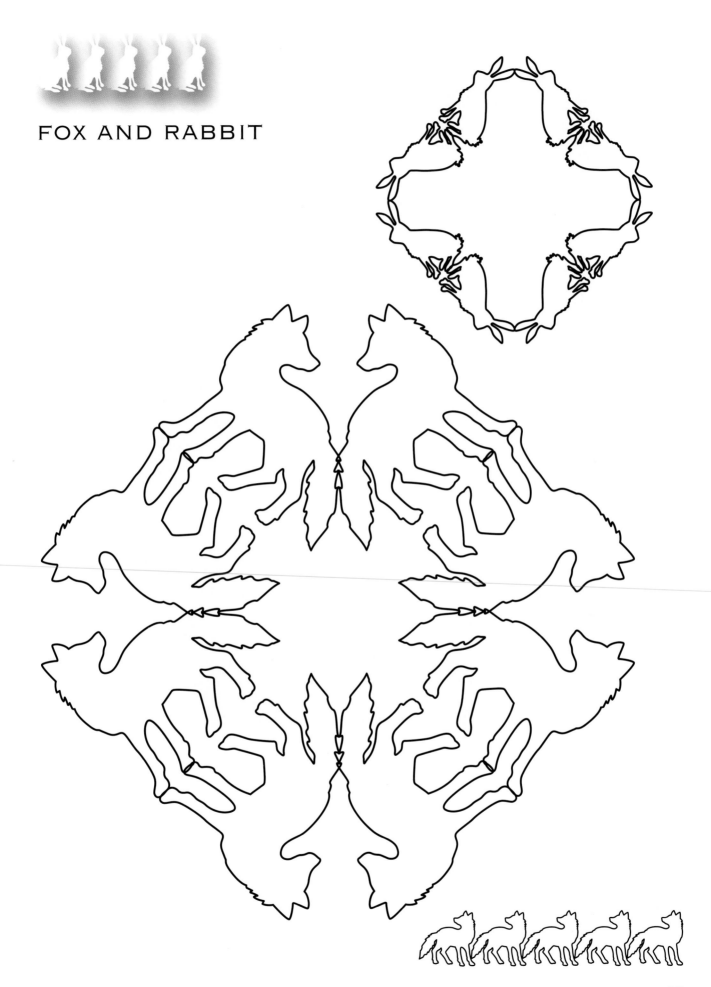

PLEASE STAY BY ME DIANA

66" x 90"

Diana monkeys are found in the coastal rain forests of west Africa from Sierra Leone to Ghana and in a small region of the Congo delta. They are one of the most endangered African primates because their habitat is being destroyed by lumbering and farming. The Edinburgh Zoo in Scotland has successfully kept and bred this species for over 17 years and has played a major roll in the conservation of the Diana monkey. I was very taken with the delicate beauty of this small monkey during my visit there in the fall of 1994.

MONKEY

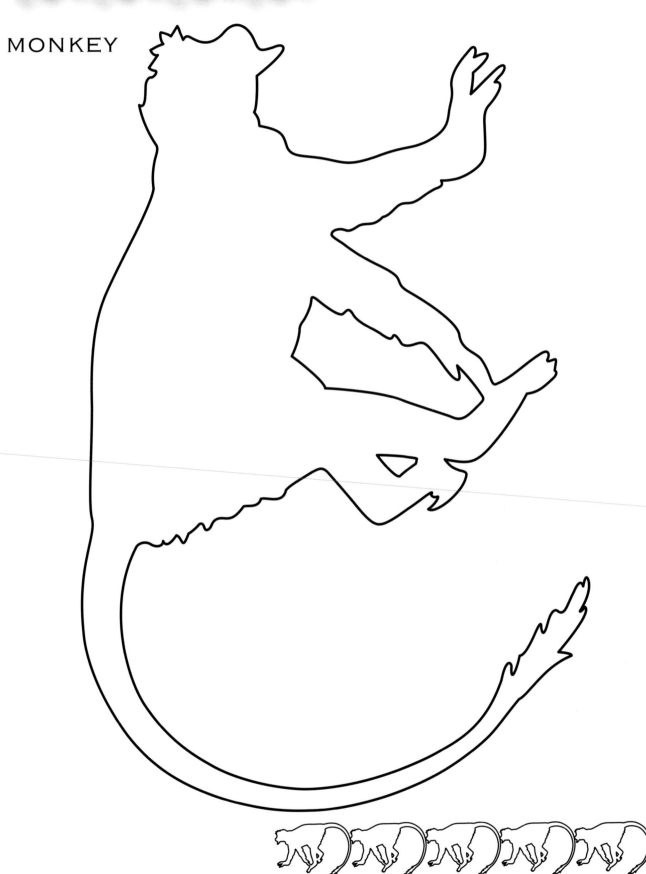

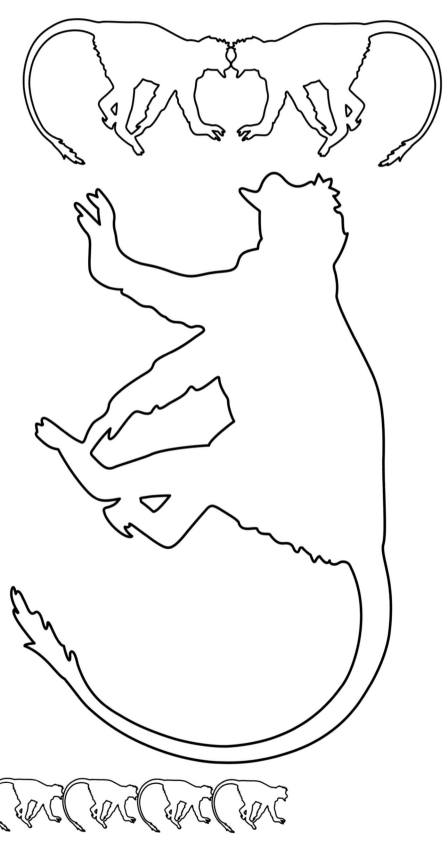

POLAR ESPRESSO

46" x 54"

Polar bears occur in areas under the jurisdiction of five nations: Russia, Norway, Denmark, Canada, and the United States. Since 1973, an agreement between these nations prohibits the use of aircraft and large motorized vessels as an aid to bear hunting. Human development, especially that associated with oil and gas exploration and extraction, poses the greatest threat to polar bear habitat. (Alaska Department of Fish and Game)

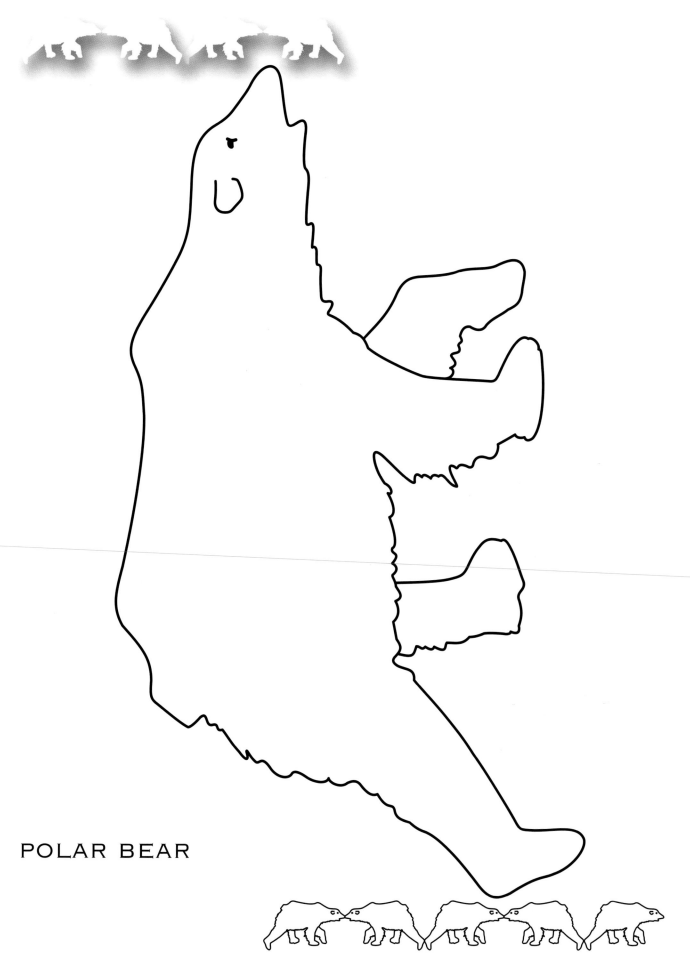

POLAR BEAR

POLAR BEAR

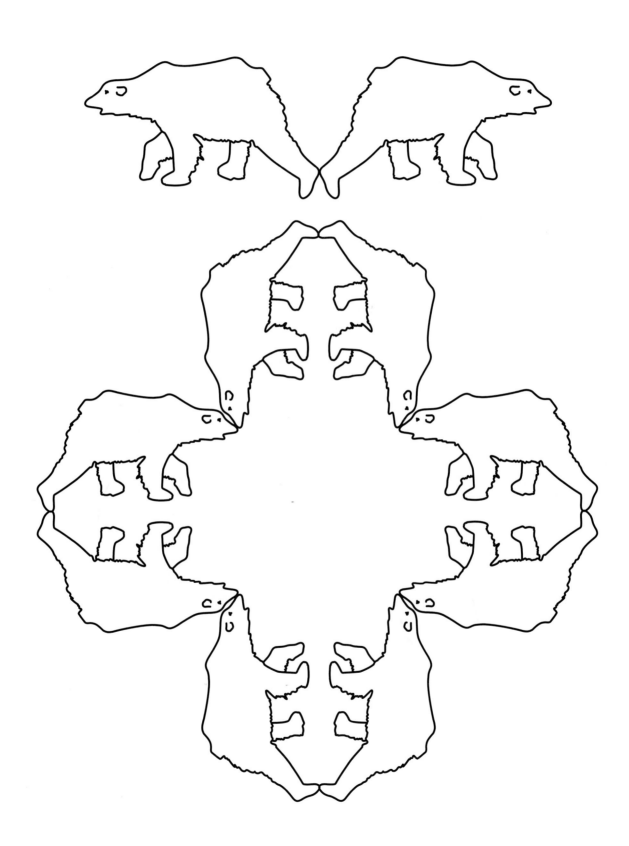

PAWS FOR THE BEAR NECESSITIES

55" x 55"

Grizzly bears epitomize the idea of wilderness. Like humans, they eat roots, fungi, plants, and mammals. A potential decline of the white bark pine, possibly caused by global warming, may mean up to 40 percent less food for bears in the future. As the bears forage for food in an expanded area, they pose a threat to humans. Bear encounters can usually be avoided if people move loudly and cautiously through grizzly habitat. (*New York Times,* Jim Robbins, January 8, 2000)

PRAIRIE DOGS

PRAIRIE DOGS

NO SAFETY IN SIBERIA

51" x 56"

The Siberian tiger lives in eastern Russia, and a few are found in northeastern China and northern North Korea. They are critically endangered. A male Siberian tiger can weigh as much as 350 kg, or 770 lbs., making it the largest cat in the world. Their major threat comes from poachers because tiger bones, skins, and organs are used in traditional Asian medicines. In an unstable and worsening economy, killing tigers is a new enterprise. Many conservation agencies are promoting efforts to assist Russia in stopping the poaching. (*Newsweek,* January 18, 1993)

TIGERS

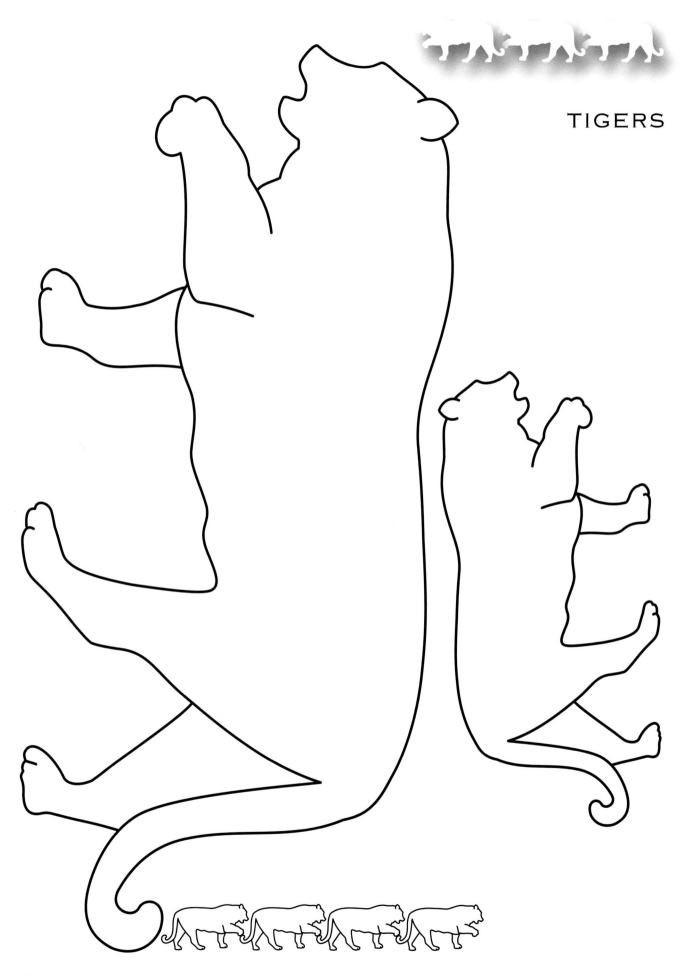

TIGERS

WOLVES AT THE DOOR

41" x 49"

In years past ranchers nearly eliminated predators from all or parts of their natural range in Wyoming. Only after these animals had almost disappeared did we begin to understand the consequences of our actions and the need to restore them to their natural habitats. Now, after many years of opposition, public sentiment generally supports the re-introduction of the gray wolf to the Yellowstone ecosystem. Controversy now centers on how the wolves should be managed when they stray from park boundaries.

WOLVES

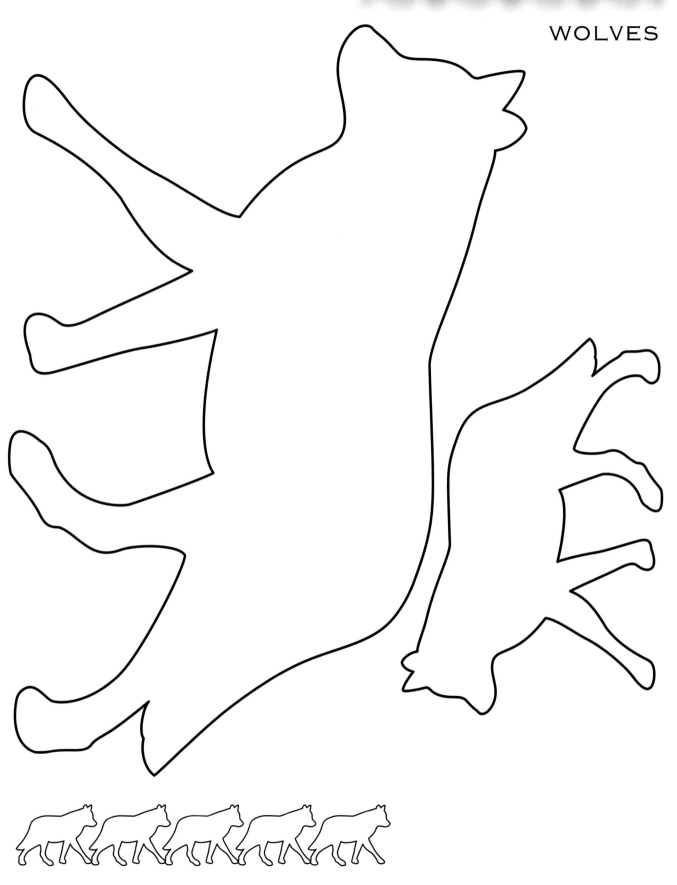

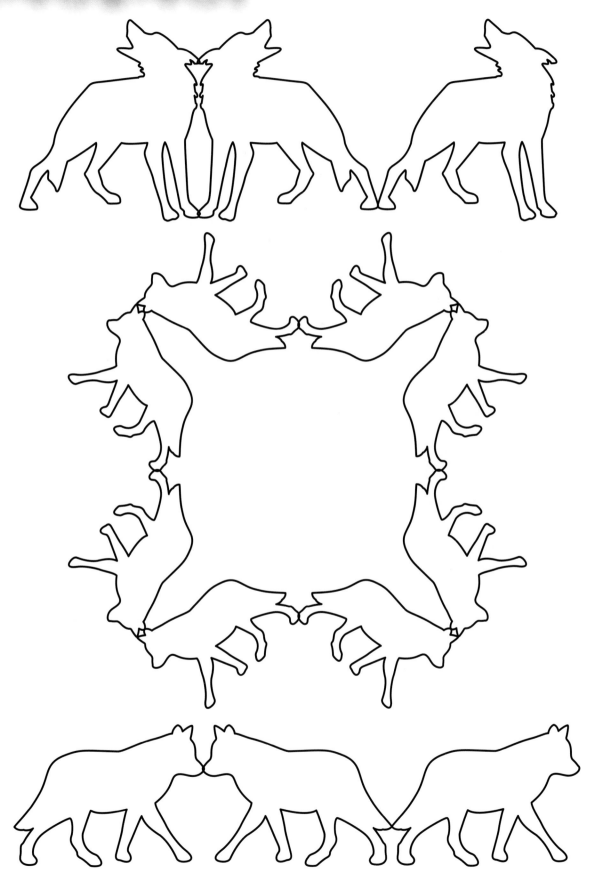

WALLABIES WANNABE

46" x 45"

The yellow-footed rock wallaby was once hunted for sport in Australia. In recent years, predation by feral red foxes and grazing competition from introduced goats and rabbits have been serious enough for this subspecies to be classified as rare. A long-term aim is to use vermin-proof fences in selected wallaby habitat and eradicate the feral animals within the fences. (Earth Sanctuaries Limited http://fp.dev-com.com/earthrockwal.htm)

WALLABY

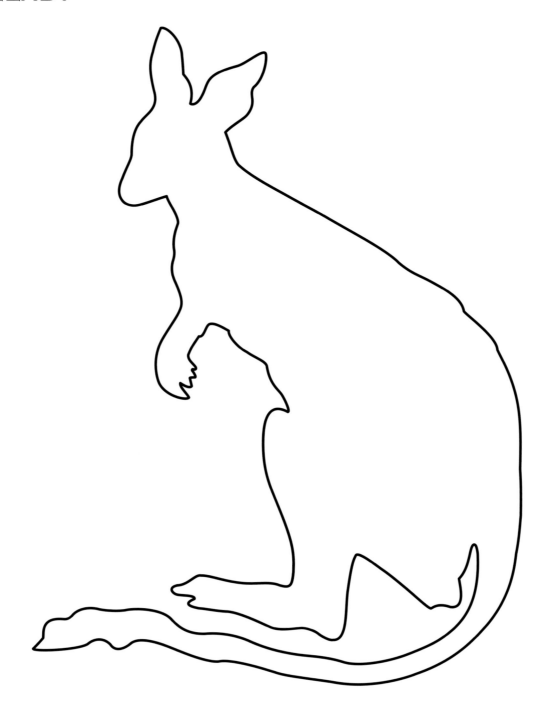

WALLABY

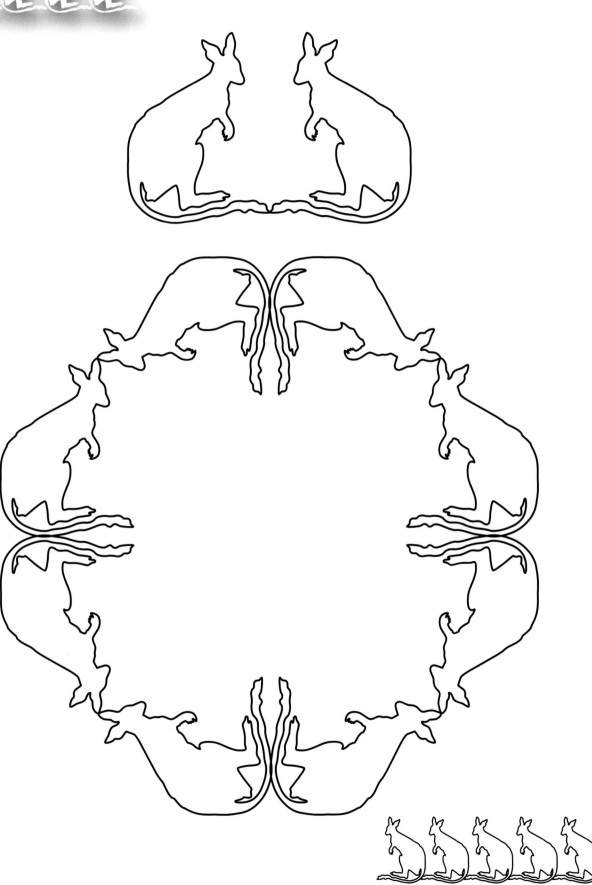

ADIOS AMIGOS: HOLA MEXICO!

59" x 52"

In October 2001 two dozen endangered captive-bred black-footed ferrets were released by the U.S. Fish and Wildlife Service, near Janos, Chihuahua, Mexico. Biologists believe that the Janos site offers one of the best opportunities to re-establish a self-sustaining population of black-footed ferrets in the largest remaining disease-free prairie dog colony in North America. Thought to be extinct in 1979, a small colony of 129 ferrets was discovered in a prairie dog town near Meeteetse, Wyoming, in 1981. When the Meeteetse group was nearly wiped out by sylvatic plaque and canine distemper in 1987, the remaining 18 ferrets were moved to a captive breeding facility in Laramie. Black-footed ferret decline and near extinction are a direct result of fewer prairie dogs in the historic habitats. Today, there are 700 black-footed ferrets in existence with about half of those living in the wild.

FERRET

FERRET

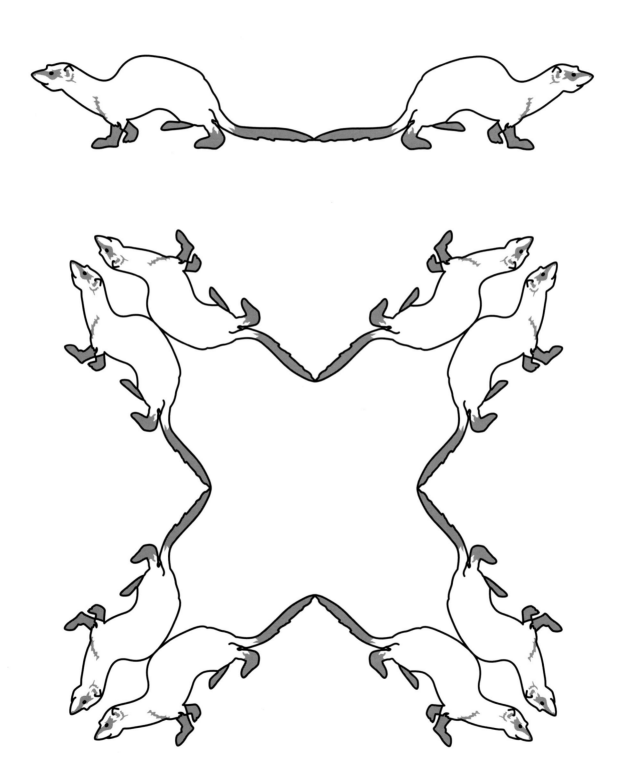

ADDITIONAL PATTERNS

LOGGERHEAD LAMBADA

It is estimated that less than one percent of sea turtles survives to maturity. To increase their survival rate, each year since 1989, turtle excluder devices have been used on U.S. shrimp boat nets to save up to 400,000 turtles from drowning. In addition, volunteers in Mexico and the U.S. patrol beaches during nesting season to enhance sea turtle safety. (Vancouver Aquarium Marine Science website) PHOTO: MARTA AMUNDSON

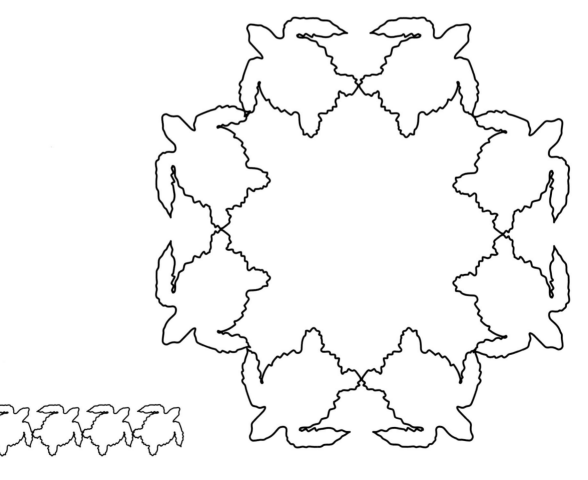

CROW

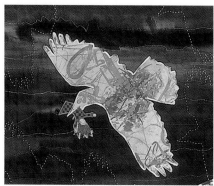

DREAMSCAPE 2, detail
(See full quilt on page 120.)

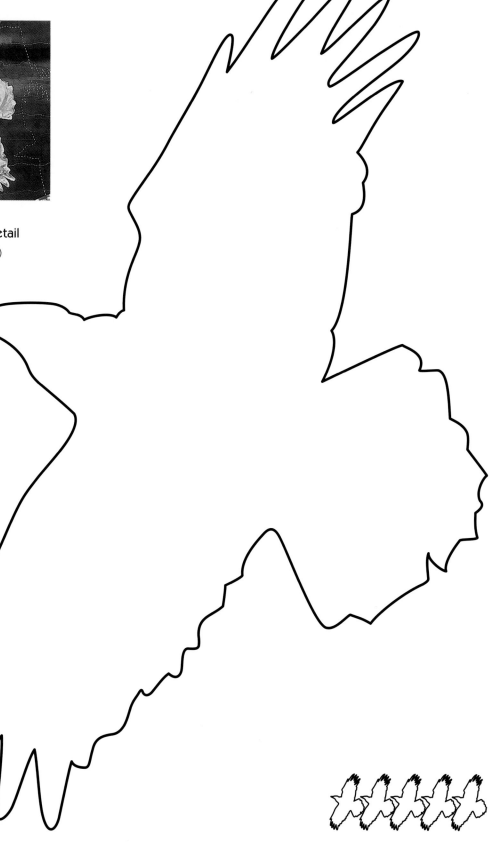

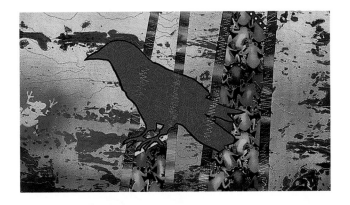

RAVEN

MINNESOTA MUTANTS

A group of students from the Minnesota New County School and their teacher, Cindy Reinitz, made the initial discovery during a nature studies class the first week of August 1995. Researchers found frogs at 100 sites in 54 of the state's 87 counties, with missing legs, extra legs, and missing eyes. At first scientists thought that the mutations were caused by environmental toxins, but later they discovered that trematodes (a kind of flat worm the size of a pin head) were causing the deformities. *Washington Post*

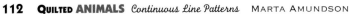

GORILLA

TWINS

Twin lowland gorillas were born at the Bronx Zoo in early January 1995. Their mother Pattycake was paired with Timmy, a male on loan from one of the 51 zoos in North America which participate in a program for captive breeding. The goal of these zoos is to share their gene pools and stop the taking of endangered animals from their homes in the wild.

PHOTO: MARTA AMUNDSON

DON'T WALK UNDER LADDERS

While predators were once considered pests, they are now thought of as a natural and even essential part of the ecosystem. In fact, because coyotes eat mostly rodents and not sheep, farmers say that leaving the coyotes alone helps reduce rodent problems on their land. Wolves and coyotes are essential to the Yellowstone ecosystem if nature is to restore the balance between elk and buffalo, and the available grazing land needed to nourish their swelling numbers. (Thoreau Institute, Randal O'Toole, 1994). PHOTO: MARTA AMUNDSON

COYOTE

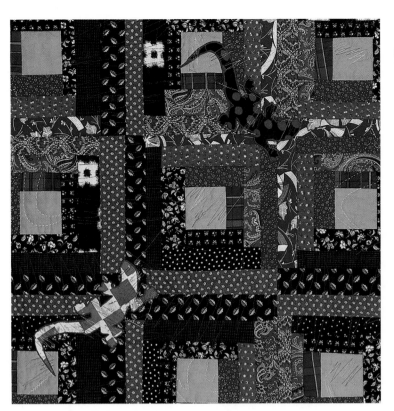

VARIETY IS THE SPICE OF LIFE

Each year on Earth Day, I start a traditional quilt from scraps in my studio. It gives me pleasure to renew, reuse, and recycle materials that might otherwise be thrown away. While making this quilt, I think about my new work and how I can make it speak to enhance the public education about endangered animals and fragile environments.

SALAMANDER

TOAD TERRIFIC

43" x 49"

The Wyoming Toad is found only in Albany County near Laramie. Thought to be extinct in the wild in 1994, the toads have made an amazing comeback due to the efforts of the U.S. Fish and Wildlife Service and the Wyoming Game and Fish Department. After a seven-year program of captive breeding, they are reproducing on their own and repopulating their former range around Mortensen, George, and Rush lakes. (*Wyoming Wildlife*)

RED CHAIR...BLUE RHINO

46" x 59"

The decline of natural habitats and other threats to wildlife mean it will be necessary for mankind to manage nature in order to save it. Despite anti-poaching measures in the wild, the black rhinoceros could be extinct by the end of the century. Through captive breeding and continuing public education, it may be possible for zoos to save rhinos and other endangered animals from extinction. (London Zoo)

DREAMSCAPE 2: EVERY PICTURE TELLS A STORY

58" x 58"

I made this quilt from the images in a dream in anticipation of my 1994 lecture/workshop tour in Scotland. My students all had a good time guessing how the figures were related. I asked them to sign their names in the pink and white squares. Now when I read these names, I can see their faces.

ON THE THRESHOLD OF A LIE: THE ARTIST CELEBRATES 40 YEARS

45" x 46"

It was the year of my fortieth birthday when I made this second signature quilt. I started to worry about my life being half over, so I asked a girlfriend if she wasn't worried too, and we set off for the Sphinx. We sailed down the Nile and rode camels in the desert. I cried when 17 tourists were murdered by the Islamic jehad on the steps of the hotel where we had slept three nights before. We rode donkeys into the Valley of the Kings at sunrise and saw the tomb of King Tut. We carefully avoided all the men with assault rifles but made friends with the children in the streets. All in all, it was a wonderful journey I will never forget.

PINEAPPLE PIE

64" x 64"

Hawaii is the extinction capital of the United States, claiming roughly one-third of the endangered species in the entire country. In the past two centuries, approximately 40 percent of Hawaii's native bird species have become extinct. There is a very serious problem with introduced alien plant and animal species that are taking over the habitats of native flora and fauna. Feral pigs, goats, sheep, ants, and domestic cattle join forces with mongooses, mosquitoes, and men to take their unfair share of the Pineapple Pie.

PUSS IN THE CORNER

47" x 45"

Bengal tigers are found throughout India from the Himalayas to Cape Comorin. Their numbers have dwindled to 4,000 from 100,000 a century ago. Range depletion and black market traffic in tiger hide and bones for traditional Asian medicine have created a crisis for the world's remaining wild tigers. Eco-tourism can provide a financial incentive to protect tigers in India's nine national parks. A primary concern in these parks is building a prey base. With enough to eat, enough space, and sufficient protection from poachers, Bengal tigers can again flourish. (*National Geographic,* December 1997)

HANNIBAL'S LAMENT

66" x 71"

A combination of ivory poaching and loss of habitat has reduced the African elephant population from 1,300,000 in 1979 to an estimated 608,000 in 1989. Even if ivory poaching can be controlled, increasing human population and resulting habitat loss pose a great challenge for conservationists in their efforts to save the remaining elephants.

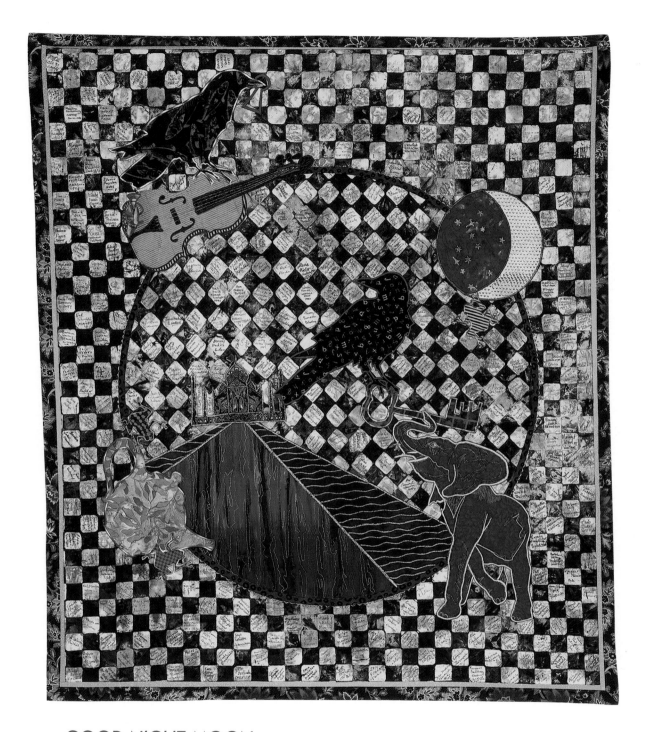

GOOD NIGHT MOON

44" x 49"

Dreams are shaped by our individual character and experiences. By paying attention to the messages given to us in sleep, we can open up to self-discovery. I dream of faraway places and somehow find a way to make my dreams come true. This quilt is signed by quilters and friends I met on my 1997 lecture tour in Denmark, Germany, Sweden, and England. Quilting continues to help me fulfill my life ambition to go to exotic places and meet interesting people. Two years after I made this quilt, I went to India and lived out another dream.

NIGHT FLIGHT TO FLORENCE

33" x 32"

Linear perspective was invented by Filippo Brunelleschi in about 1413. A recent dream I had included Brunelleschi's perspective demonstration of the Palazzo de Signori in Florence. It is difficult for me to understand my dreams even when I have a clear visual memory of all the elements. I can only guess that, because I live on a ranch that is seven metal cattle guards from civilization, my mind treats me to imagined travel when I need it most. A good night journey can restore my sense of well being just when life is most arduous and demanding.

LOOSE LIPS SINK SHIPS

24" x 24"

This quilt was made for all the journalists and bureaucrats who told more than we ever wanted to know during President Clinton's second term in office. The quilt toured for two years in a trunk show for the Quilter's Guild of the British Isles.

ABOUT THE AUTHOR

Marta Amundson is a wildlife advocate and professional quiltmaker who exhibits throughout the United States and abroad. She writes articles on quilting for books and magazines in the United States, Sweden, Australia, and Britain. Known as the "Quilting Cowgirl," she teaches innovative machine quilting techniques around the world. She was chosen in 1995 and 2002 to receive a Wyoming Arts Council Fellowship and won the grand prize in the 2001 American Folk Art Museum International Competition.

The author earned a bachelor of arts degree in visual art and art history from Albion College in Michigan and has an associate degree of science from Central Wyoming College.

In addition to her passion for fly fishing, Marta is an avid skier. She also likes to kayak, bike, and scuba dive. She often travels to exotic places to view and photograph endangered animals as inspiration for the drawings on her quilts.

OTHER AQS BOOKS

This is only a small selection of the books available from the American Quilter's Society. AQS books are known worldwide for timely topics, clear writing, beautiful color photos, and accurate illustrations and patterns. The following books are available from your local bookseller, quilt shop, or public library.

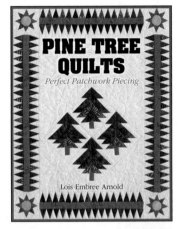

PINE TREE QUILTS
Perfect Patchwork Piecing
Lois Embree Arnold

#5708   us$22.95

Helen's Copy & Use Quilting Patterns
HELEN SQUIRE

#6006   us$25.95

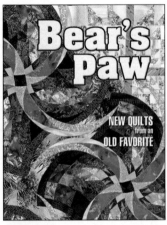

Bear's Paw
NEW QUILTS from an OLD FAVORITE

#5754   us$19.95

NO DRAGONS ON MY QUILT
by Jean Ray Laury with Ritva Laury and Lizabeth Laury

REVISED EDITION

#5794   us$16.95

Add-a-Line
Continuous QUILTING Patterns
Janie Donaldson

#6069   us$24.95

Embroidered **Childhood MEMORIES**
Brenna Hopkins & Nori Koenig

#6008   us$19.95

Quilted Havens
CITY HOUSES, COUNTRY HOMES
Susan Purney-Mark & Daphne Greig

#5336   us$22.95

Cutting CURVES from STRAIGHT PIECES
Debbie Bowles

#5755   us$21.95

FOUNDATION BORDERS Hall & Haywood
Jane Hall & Dixie Haywood

#6075   us$24.95

LOOK FOR THESE BOOKS NATIONALLY OR CALL 1-800-626-5420